P9-APC-652

ARMOURED
FIREPOWER

ARMOURED FIREPOWER

LINDSAY PEACOCK

Published by Salamander Books Limited
LONDON • NEW YORK

A Salamander Book

Published by Salamander Books Ltd.
129-137 York Way,
London N7 9LG,
United Kingdom.

ISBN 0 86101 520 7

Distributed in the United Kingdom by:
Hodder and Stoughton Services,
PO Box 6,
Mill Road,
Dunton Green,
Sevenoaks.
Kent TN13 2XX

Designed by Paul Johnson
and the Maltings Partnership

Filmset by The Old Mill, London

Colour Reproduction by Scantrans Pte, Singapore

Printed and bound in Spain

Photo Credits
Jacket: (front) UK MoD, (back) US DoD, **Endpapers:** US DoD, **Page 1:** Jeremy Flack/API, **2/3:** Jeremy Flack/API, **4/5:** US DoD, **6/7:** US Army, **8:** John Norris, **9:** US Army, **10:** (top) UKLF, (bottom) US DoD, **11:** UKLF, **12/13:** US DoD, **14/15:** US DoD, **16/17:** US DoD, **18:** US Army, **19:** Rafael, **20/21:** US Army, **22/23:** US Army, **24/25:** Jeremy Flack/API, **26/27:** UKLF, **28/29:** (top right) Jeremy Flack/API, (rest) UKLF, **30/31:** US Army, **32/33:** (bottom left) Jeremy Flack/API, (rest) US DoD, **34/35:** (left) GIAT, (rest) John Norris, **36/37:** (clockwise, from top left) Armscor, Dutch MoD, UKLF, Danish Army, **38/39:** Engesa, **40/41:** Jeremy Flack/API, **42/43:** (bottom right) GIAT, (rest) Panhard, **44/45:** (top left) Oerlikon, (top right) Mowag, (bottom) G.M. Canada, **46/47:** Steyr, **48/49:** Armscor, **50/51:** (left) US DoD, (rest) US Army, **52/53:** (clockwise, from top left) US DoD, US Army, Hughes, McDD, **54/55:** GKN, **56/57:** (top left) Oerlikon, (rest) US DoD, **58/59:** (top right) Mowag, (rest) GM Canada, **60/61:** (top right) Jeremy Flack/API, (rest) US DoD, **62/63:** US DoD, **64/65:** Armscor, **66/67:** US DoD, **68/69:** US DoD, **70/71:** (left) Quadrant Picture Library, (rest) Hughes, **72/73:** Jeremy Flack/API, **74/75:** US Army, **76/77:** IMI, **78/79:** Armscor, **80/81:** US DoD, **82/83:** (left) Gamma, (right) French MoD, **84/85:** (top left) US Army, (rest) US DoD, **86/87:** US Army, **88/89:** (bottom left) US DoD, (bottom right) Bofors, (rest) US Army, **90/91:** Hughes, **92/93:** Jeremy Flack/API, **94/95:** (top left) MBB, (top right) Mowag, (rest) Euromissile, **96/97:** (left) US DoD, (top right) USMC, (bottom right) McDD, **98/99:** (bottom left) Aerospatiale, (top right) Euromissile, (rest) MBB, **100/101:** Bofors, **102/103:** US DoD, **104/105:** McDD, **106/107:** (top left) Jeremy Flack/API, (top right) John Norris, (bottom) US Army, **108/109:** Martin Marietta, **110/111:** Euromissile, **112/113:** (top left) MBB, (rest) Hughes, **114/115:** (top right) Mowag, (bottom right) Matra, (rest) Thomson CSF, **116/117:** (top left) US DoD, (right) Ford, **118/119:** US Army, **120/121:** (top right) UK MoD, (rest) BAe, **122/123:** (clockwise from top) BAe, UK MoD, US DoD, **124/125:** US Army, **126/127:** Matra, **128/129:** US DoD, **130/131:** US DoD, **132/133:** (bottom left) GM Canada, (rest) GE, **134/135:** US DoD, **136/137:** US DoD, **138/139:** US DoD, **140/141:** Jeremy Flack/API, **142/143:** US DoD, **144/145:** US DoD, **146/147:** US DoD, **148/149:** Jeremy Flack/API, **150/151:** US DoD, **152/153:** Jeremy Flack /API, **154/155:** (bottom left) Rafael,(rest) US DoD, **156/157:** US DoD, **158:** Oerlikon.

Endpapers: M60A3 in desert exercise
Page 1: Chieftain main battle tank
2/3: Challenger tank on exercise
4/5: M2 Bradleys on the move
6/7: M1 Abrams emitting screening smoke
8: (top) Scorpion light tank driver
9: M1 Abrams at speed
10: Scorpion in winter camouflage; (bottom) launching a Tow anti-tank missile
11: Tracked Rapier anti-aircraft system

INTRODUCTION

As WITH OTHER AREAS of warfare the ground battlefield has witnessed a considerable amount of change during the past few decades. Motivated in part by the relentless progress of technology and the advent of new tactics and weapons, the modern soldier is more likely to ride to war aboard an armoured personnel carrier or even a helicopter rather than march into battle, as was the case in the past.

Mobility is perhaps the single most important factor in bringing about this change, with Germany's expertise in the "Blitzkrieg" (Lightning War) philosophy of World War II emphatically pointing the way ahead.

At that time, it was indeed a most revolutionary way of conducting war on the ground, with the skilful employment of tanks, artillery and aerial firepower in conjunction with fast-moving "shock" troops enabling Hitler's Third Reich to establish military dominance over much of Europe in a surprisingly short time. Faced with that doctrine and lacking the tools to stall the Wehrmacht offensive, the Allied nations were overwhelmed in a matter of weeks.

The lessons that were so forcibly driven home in the German onslaught have provided the basis for ground warfare doctrine ever since and mobility is very much the watchword today, some 50 years later. Thus, tanks, armoured cars, self-propelled artillery and armoured personnel carriers all feature strongly in the composition of a modern army. So do helicopters, with the rotary-wing flying machine being perhaps the most exciting

addition of recent times. Regarded almost as a fast land vehicle, the low-flying helicopter is able to move troops quickly from point to point or to bring devastating firepower to bear on, for instance, an enemy armoured column.

Notwithstanding the developments in army aviation, this volume is firmly focussed on the ground-based elements which embrace various types of armoured fighting vehicle as well as self-propelled artillery pieces and anti-aircraft and battlefield missiles such as those designed specifically for the "tank-busting" task.

One only has to look at the tank to see that it has changed virtually beyond recognition since it was first employed in combat in 1916. While still fundamentally nothing more than a "mobile gun", the tank has benefitted from the provision of ever more accurate aiming devices, which have progressively raised the "first-hit" probability rate. The laser is the most recent of these aids to find widespread acceptance and is, not surprisingly, far superior to anything that has gone before. When used in conjunction with a ballistic fire-control computer, it has enabled the "first-hit" probability rate to increase to around the 90 per cent mark. That highly impressive figure is, of course, unlikely to be achieved on a fluid battlefield amidst the clamour of war but there can be little doubt that tank crews who expose their vehicle to hostile fire would surely be viewed as a bad risk by life assurance salesmen.

The most lethal anti-armour projectile is the Armour Piercing Fin-Stabilised Discarding Sabot (APFSDS), a tungsten or depleted uranium dart propelled at over half a mile a second to cut through the thickest armour plate. High-Explosive Squash Head (HESH) is another type, this crumpling on impact and then detonating to cause scabs of armour to detach from the tank interior with devastating consequences for anything or anyone inside. High-Explosive Anti-Tank (HEAT) is yet another, the hollow-charge warhead being designed to direct a jet of gas and molten metal through the tank hull, again with dire consequences. And, of course, there are other more conventional shells such as fragmentation and high explosive which could be used to deadly effect against "soft" targets like infantry.

Such improvements in accuracy and kill probability are by no means one-sided

and they have spawned ever greater efforts at enhancing the tank's survivability. For a time, this was achieved by simply increasing the thickness of the armour plate. It was an effective solution up to a point but did mean that the tank's weight also rose and the benefits were soon swallowed up by penalties in terms of range, speed and manoeuvrability.

Compound and reactive armour were two solutions to the desire for greater protection, with the latter possessing perhaps slightly greater versatility in that it can be simply "bolted on" to an existing tank. Each has its advantages and disadvantages but both types confer a good measure of protection against a variety of anti-tank munitions and the weight penalty must therefore be viewed as an acceptable one.

Nevertheless, there are those who argue that the main battle tank is now in grave danger of becoming an unnecessary luxury and it is certainly true that an impressive array of fire power can now be brought to bear against these battlefield heavyweights. Missiles must surely pose the greatest threat and most armies now feature weapons of this kind in their composition although not all of them are in the happy position of being able to field man-, vehicle- and helicopter-portable variations on the theme.

Arguments over the matter of vulnerability do not, however, appear to have overly impressed army hierarchies or those responsible for the procurement of hardware and the main battle tank is still far from being an endangered species, as even a cursory glance through the pages of this volume soon confirms.

Less impressively endowed in terms of firepower and weight, light tanks are also less numerous but are still quite formidable weapons in their own right. Certainly, one should not be deceived into thinking that they would necessarily be at a disadvantage in an engagement with the heavier main battle tank for many of them are compatible with anti-armour

missiles such as TOW, HOT and Milan while others may fire the full gamut of high-velocity anti-armour shells.

In a "one-on-one" engagement, the odds would clearly favour the heavier vehicle, if only by virtue of the fact that it has the ability to kill from greater range. However, an encounter of that kind presupposes that it would be able to use its superior fire-power in a "stand-off" mode and there can be no guarantee that the main battle tank would be able to engage and disengage at will. Certainly, in a skirmishing type of encounter, there can be little doubt that scavenging "packs" of light tanks could inflict serious damage on a main battle tank force, making use of their superior speed and manoeuvrability to harass an enemy.

The humble foot-soldier has also benefited from the mobility and protection provided by armoured vehicles, and the infantrymen of most armies now ride into battle in tracked or wheeled Armoured Personnel Carriers (APC). Once a simple "battle taxi", today's APC is being armed with a diverse range of light cannon, machine guns and even anti-tank missiles, hence the current terminology of "Infantry Fighting Vehicle" (IFV).

A new trend is the "family" concept, where the same basic chassis, powerplant and suspension is used with a range of specialist hulls and equipment to provide the full gamut of land warfare capability with the minimum of training, logistic and cost problems. Taking Britain's CVR(T) family as an example, while all embody a common aluminium-armoured hull, suspension and Jaguar 4.2-litre engine, the many versions that exist rely on different armament and equipment. Scorpion is fitted with a 76mm gun and could best be described as a light tank, being reasonably well equipped to look after itself in battle since it can fire HESH rounds. The close reconnaissance Scimitar is perhaps less self-reliant, by virtue of its firepower being confined to a 30mm Rarden cannon but it could sometimes operate in concert with Striker — the dedicated tank-buster. Armed with Swingfire anti-armour missiles — five in an elevating launcher at the rear and five internally-carried reloads — Striker deliberately bears a marked resemblance to Scimitar so as to confuse enemy tank crews who would obviously prefer to eliminate the threat to themselves by destroying Striker before turning their attentions to Scimitar.

Other members of the Scorpion family comprise Spartan, which is a genuine APC; Sultan, which is a battlefield command and control vehicle; Samson, which is used for engineering and recovery tasks and Samaritan, which, as its name so very clearly implies, is an ambulance.

Moving on, there is conventional artillery, the big gun still providing the heavy firepower to a modern army, although its relative lack of mobility is hardly conducive to effective operation in fast-moving situations. That is one reason why

modern armies have been increasingly switching to self-propelled guns and artillery rockets such as the Multiple Launch Rocket System (MLRS) which is based on the chassis of an extensively modified M2 Bradley mechanised infantry combat vehicle.

Capable of carrying a maximum of 12 solid-fuel missiles, each with a range of over 18 miles and able to be fired either singly or in ripple salvo for maximum shock effect, MLRS is compatible with a variety of warhead types including the very latest generation of so-called "smart" shells.

Conventional artillery pieces are also being given increased mobility and protection by mounting them on tracked armoured chassis. Such units have the enviable capability to "shoot and scoot", to fire their mission then exit the area rapidly before the inevitable counter-battery fire arrives. Linked to computerised survey, navigation and fire-control equipment, the modern artillery system bestows the commander with the ability to destroy targets virtually anywhere in the battle area.

While the advances in technology are certainly impressive, one must not lose sight of the qualities needed by the men who would be called upon to fight any future conflict. Technical skills and education are essential to gain the full benefits from sophisticated equipment — but these are not in themselves enough to withstand the stresses of the battlefield. In the final analysis it is the courage and dedication of the ordinary soldier, whether riflemen, gunner, driver, pilot, technician or operator, that makes the armoured firepower of today possible.

Pictured during the course of an all arms live-firing exercise in Germany, these two views portray the rather squat profile of the M1 Abrams main battle tank to advantage, a profile which makes it hard to see and, hopefully, even harder to hit. They also show that some of the narrow roads to be found in this part of the world are not exactly ideal for the rapid movement of armoured vehicles although had these tanks been called upon to participate in a real "shooting match", paved roads are just about the last place that one would find them.

The bed of a stream provides an almost ideal highway for an M1 Abrams and makes for a particularly striking picture as it hurries towards the scene of the action during military manoeuvres. Deep inside the hull, the tank's gunner is confronted by a most impressive collection of "switchology" and high-tech kit, all of which is designed to ensure that first shot hit. In the high-speed world of armoured conflict, he who shoots first, wins.

With spent shell cases lying around, a US Army M1 Abrams main battle tank dramatically reveals the heavyweight punch of its 105mm primary gun armament in a spectacular night study of a live firing exercise. The later M1A1 Abrams is armed with a 120mm gun, but both versions are capable of punching out an average of eight shells per minute. The Abrams also incorporates Chobham composite armour which offers a superb degree of protection against all warhead types.

One of the most widely used MBTs in the west is the USA's M60 which equips combat units of the US Army in addition to some 20 other armies around the world. The definitive and most numerous model is now the M60A3 which has a 105mm gun as its main weapon and a US Army example of this sub-type can be seen at left with its turret almost reversed as it fires a pyrotechnic simulator charge. In the view above, a modified Israeli M60 can be seen, one notable feature of this tank being the "Blazer" reactive armour panels. Offering extra protection from HEAT rounds, these consist of "sandwiches" of explosive which detonate when hit by an incoming shell in order to negate the deadly penetrative potential of this type of warhead.

Seen in action by night at an Army firing range located at Grafenwohr, West Germany, an element of M60A2 main battle tanks use their 152mm guns to bombard a target. Compatible with the Shillelagh anti-tank missile and more conventional ammunition, the M60A2 lacked the ability to fire on the move and has now been retired from service but not before it made history as being the first US MBT able to use both types of armament. In its stead, the M60A3 derivative is still in widespread use although this relies on a 105mm gun as its prime weapon system.

2424

Entering service way back in the early 1950s, the M48 has demonstrated good longevity and adaptability, progressive updating being responsible for it remaining an effective weapon up to the present day. At left is the kind of view an opponent would be anxious to avoid while below is a US Army M48A5 using local cover and foliage to advantage while engaged in manoeuvres in Korea. The later M60 was developed from the M48 and the strong resemblance can be seen in the view at the bottom left.

A line of Chieftain tanks of a British Army unit sit idle, their slightly elevated 120mm guns draped with camouflage netting and turned to face to the rear (left). Elsewhere, a Chieftain's bulky form stands out as it is silhouetted by a falling flare during a night exercise (above) while the crew of a Challenger pause by the roadside, with the driver clearly visible beneath the thermally-blanketed barrel of the 120mm gun (above left).

Fast supplanting Chieftain as the British Army's principal main battle tank, Challenger relies for its firepower on a 120mm L11A5 gun although this is to give way to a new high pressure gun in the not too distant future. Incorporating Chobham armour, it carries a crew of four and possesses a laser rangefinder as well as thermal imaging equipment to give passive day and night vision capability. The illustrations here show Challenger making good use of forest cover as it awaits the call to battle during a field exercise (far left) and breasting rising ground in a most impressive fashion (left). Finally, the view above shows something of the stress and strain of commanding a tank in action as a camouflage daubed Challenger commander peruses a map while deciding on his course of action.

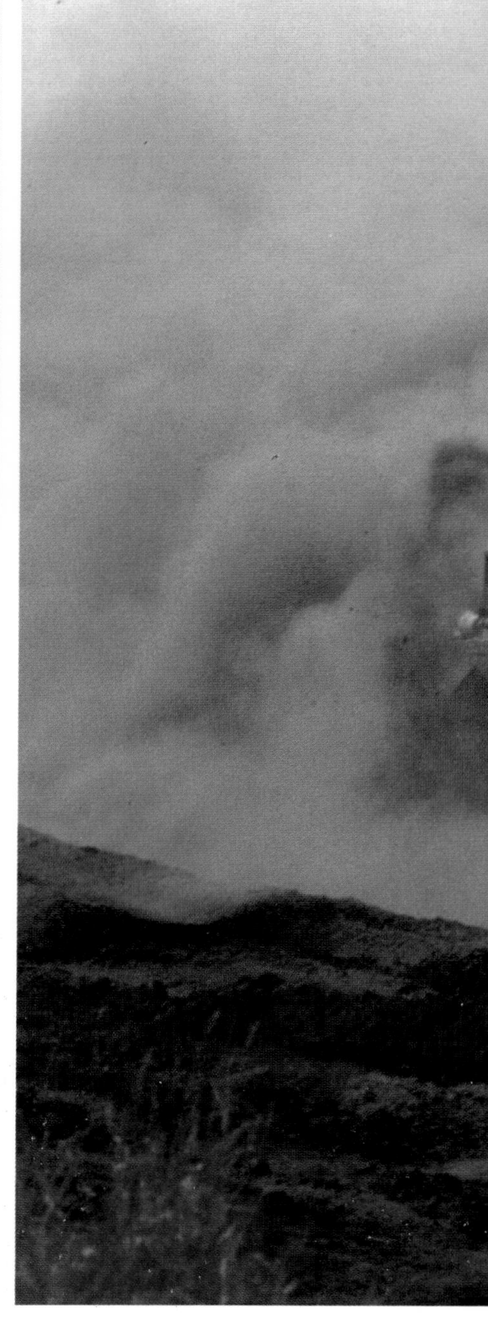

Entering service with units of the British Army more than two decades ago, Chieftain is still in widespread use today with its 120mm gun able to fire a variety of types of shell, including HESH and APFSDS. Portrayed here are a pair of standard tanks, the tank above featuring a crew in nuclear, biological and chemical warfare protective "noddy" suits while another (right) throws up an impressive cloud of dust as it moves across country at high speed. Finally, top right shows a modified tank in orange exercise markings with "stillbrew" add-on armour on the turret front.

04EB04

Fitted with a British-designed 105mm gun able to fire both armour-piercing and high-explosive squash-head shells, West Germany's Leopard 1 is still a most potent tank even though it has been in service with the Bundeswehr since 1965. Finding favour at both home and abroad, it provided a basis for several variations, these including bridgelaying and recovery vehicles in addition to the Gepard self-propelled anti-aircraft gun. Those portrayed here are standard main battle tanks, the camouflage-bedecked one on the left being an example from the Bundeswehr while the later models below are Belgian machines. Close study reveals notable differences, with the German example being fitted with a dual white light/infra-red searchlight device and pyrotechnics unit for a laser-based combat simulator.

The Leopard 1 has also proved popular with other elements of the NATO alliance and some 5,000 examples of the MBT have been built. Belgian Army Leopards are shown here with hasty snow camouflage, demonstrating the need to adapt to different environmental conditions. The Leopard chassis is also used for the self-propelled Gepard air defence weapon system (left).

32

The 105mm-armed AMX 30 tank (above and below) has been in French army service for many years. The new AMX 40 (left) with improved fire control and a heavier 120mm gun has been designed for export and should repeat the success of its older stablemate.

A British Army stalwart for many years, Centurion still fulfils a front-line role for a number of armies around the world, with most having opted to modernise gun armament and fit a 105mm weapon. Centurion versions shown here include, clockwise from above, a South African license-built Olifant with a 105mm gun, a standard Centurion of the Dutch Army, a British Centurion AVRE with a 165mm "bunker-busting" gun and mine-clearance ploughs and a standard Centurion of the Belgian Army.

56

BLOODHOUND

When it comes to the building of main battle tanks, only a few nations are sufficiently well-endowed industrially to undertake such a venture. The superpowers naturally head the list and other countries include France, Switzerland, Italy, Germany and the United Kingdom. Brazil also has the capability and these studies depict the Osorio EE-T1 which has a 105mm gun able to fire most shell types. Fire control options include panoramic thermal sights and laser range finders and a 120mm gun can be installed. While certainly an impressive vehicle, the Osorio is yet to find an initial user either at home or abroad.

(Overleaf) Unrecognisable due to a shroud of camouflage, an RAF Regiment Scorpion keeps a watching brief over dispersed site operations, as, in the background, a Harrier GR.5 is readied for another sortie from the protection of its net-draped hide in West Germany.

Conceived primarily for the export market, France's ERC90 armoured light reconnaissance vehicle has also been adopted by the French Army which took delivery of its first example in 1984. Main armament is a 90mm cannon and this vehicle is quite a sporty performer, being able to rattle along the highway at speeds of up to 100km per hour. As can be seen from the accompanying pictures, it is also fully amphibious.

W-75

Typical of the new breed of multi-role light armoured vehicles is the Swiss MOWAG Piranha. Available in eight- and six-wheeled versions it can be equipped with a vast range of weaponry. Shown here are the personnel carrier with a 25mm cannon (top left), the fire support vehicle with a 90mm gun (left) and an anti-tank version with a TOW missile turret. Both Canada and America use license-built versions of the Piranha in a multitude of roles.

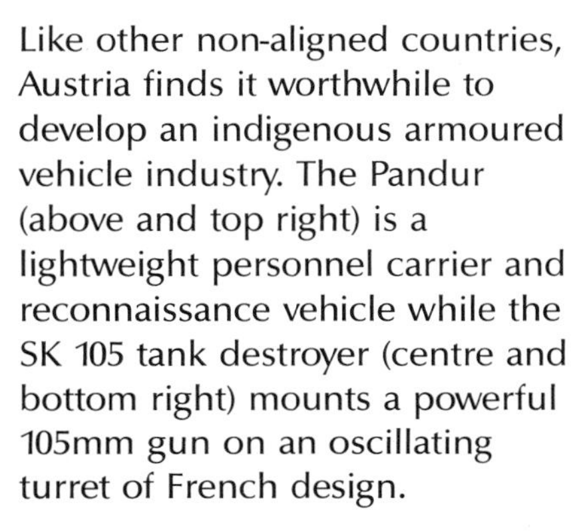

Like other non-aligned countries, Austria finds it worthwhile to develop an indigenous armoured vehicle industry. The Pandur (above and top right) is a lightweight personnel carrier and reconnaissance vehicle while the SK 105 tank destroyer (centre and bottom right) mounts a powerful 105mm gun on an oscillating turret of French design.

R127057

Barred from many of the Free World's markets, South Africa has had little option but to go it alone and develop much of its own hardware, a policy which has allowed its armed forces to buy equipment that is very closely tailored to their own requirements. The Rooikat combat reconnaissance vehicle depicted here is one such indigenous product and has a 76mm cannon able to fire six APFSDS or HE shells a minute as its main weapon. Examples of the Rooikat are seen here in typical African terrain (left and far left) and crossing a minefield when under test (below).

Able to carry seven infantry in addition to its three-man crew, the M2/3 Bradley is now in the process of supplanting the M113 as the main APC with combat units of the US Army. Much better equipped than the M113 to look after itself on the battlefield, the Bradley is well-armoured and fully amphibious. The transported infantry can fire from weapon ports in the hull and when dismounted use the full range of infantry anti-personnel and anti-armour weapons.

Able to carry seven troops in addition to its three-man crew, the M2 Bradley packs quite a powerful punch, its armament array comprising a 25mm Bushmaster Chain Gun, a 7.62mm co-axial machine gun and a two-cell TOW anti-tank missile launcher. It is also fully amphibious once the flotation screen has been erected and recent production examples have acquired extra protection through provision of reactive armour. Another model, optimised for service with US Cavalry regiments, is the M3 but this lacks firing ports for use by infantrymen.

The latest armoured personnel carrier to enter service with the British Army, Warrior has a crew of three and is able to accommodate seven infantrymen internally. Prime armament is a 30mm RARDEN cannon capable of firing armour-piercing and high explosive incendiary rounds. In conjunction with a top road speed approaching 50mph (80kph), this kind of firepower represents a quantum leap in capability and it seems set to meet with considerable success on the export market. Continuing development of the basic Warrior is leading to the appearance of new models, these including a mechanised repair and recovery vehicle, a mortar carrier, an engineer vehicle and a command post vehicle. These illustrations portray the standard Warrior APC with the main picture showing it alongside a BAOR Challenger in West Germany.

The M113 armoured personnel carrier is undoubtedly one of the USA's military successes when it comes to hardware and it spawned an impressive list of specialised variants, some of which are shown here. The main picture is of a standard APC which is able to carry up to 11 fully-equipped troops while the view at right shows an unusual variation fitted with a turret containing an Oerlikon 25mm cannon. Lastly, there is the M901 ITV or Improved TOW Vehicle which is seen below. This is fitted with a retractable launcher that can carry a pair of TOW anti-armour missiles.

76

MAC

Based on the MOWAG Piranha, the Canadian LAV-25 light armoured vehicle began life purely as a personnel carrier but has since displayed versatility by taking on new missions and equipment. Now active with the US Marines in large numbers, the basic APC is armed with a 25mm cannon, is fully amphibious and can carry six troops in addition to a three-man crew. Examples portrayed here, including one being delivered from a C-130 Hercules by means of the low-altitude parachute extraction system, are all basic APCs.

One of the great drawbacks of towed artillery is its lack of mobility and it was to overcome that deficiency that self-propelled artillery was evolved. The American M109 is one instance of this type of weapon and entered service with the US Army way back in the early 1960s. Since then, it has become the most widely used self-propelled howitzer in the world as well as one of the most potent for it can fire conventional shells and tactical nuclear warheads as well as special projectiles containing sub-munitions and the laser-homing anti-armour Copperhead. Variants of the M109 are shown here, that on the right having the early short-barrelled type of gun while the US Army and British Army examples (shown respectively at top left and right) both have the later long barrel.

00 ED71

97101
24

12FH71
AWD-50

An even more powerful gun is fitted to the American M110 self-propelled howitzer which features a 203mm (8in) weapon capable of hurling shells out as far as 15 miles (24km). In US Army service, it may fire both conventional and nuclear types of shell in addition to sub-munitions like grenades and chemical agents. A five-man crew travels with the gun itself, while the other eight members of the team use an M548 or M992 support vehicle which also carries stocks of ammunition.

South Africa's highly capable indigenous arms industry has developed some rather potent and effective weapons, which are epitomised by these items of heavy artillery. Towed G5 howitzers are shown in action at left and a variant of this gun gives a "heavy punch" to the G6 self-propelled howitzer shown above. With the ability to project a shell in excess of 18 miles (30km) with great accuracy, it is an extremely lethal weapon system as well as one that is combat proven.

Although lacking in mobility, the M198 towed field howitzer is still an essential element of US firepower and has also been adopted by several other countries. Capable of hurling standard high explosive types of shell over 13 miles (22km) and special rocket assisted projectiles out to a distance of almost 19 miles (30km), it is also compatible with the Copperhead laser-homing anti-tank munition. In the picture above, a loader is seen about to insert a red bagged charge into the breech while a high-explosive shell is clearly visible in the right foreground. With the gun crew having withdrawn to a safe distance, a lanyard is used to fire the howitzer (right), gases caused by the propellant pouring out of the muzzle as the projectile heads for its target. Initially, up to four shells per minute may be fired but sustained firing rate is only two per minute so as to prevent overheating.

One of the more unusual types of shell that may be fired by standard US Army artillery is the laser-guided Copperhead and an example of this "smart round" is shown here in the process of being loaded into a M198 gun during a military training exercise conducted in the United States.

(Overleaf) Copperhead is then fired into the general area of the target, which is being marked by a laser designator. Locking-on to laser energy reflected by the target, the shell is able to home with extreme accuracy as shown by the two views of a redundant tank being hit by Copperhead.

Shrouded by camouflage nets, examples of the British 105mm Light Gun fire in succession (above) while two members of a gun crew are shown loading a projectile as a third goes about the job of bringing it to bear on its target (right). Used in combat in the 1982 battle for the Falklands, maximum firing rate is six rounds per minute and it can hit targets up to 10 miles (17km) away. The light-gun is deployable by aircraft or helicopter and can be transported to any battle zone and committed to action in quick time.

Of contemporary battlefield weapons, without doubt one of the most spectacular has to be the Multiple Launch Rocket System portrayed here. Based on the M2 Bradley light AFV chassis, it has a dozen launch tubes, each capable of housing one 600lb (270kg) solid-fuel missile with a range that surpasses 18 miles (29km). Fired either singly or in ripple salvo, each rocket can dispense an impressive array of sub-munitions or mines, and the whole package is designed with area denial in mind. Fast, with good range and mobility, this collection of pictures show MLRS on the move, deployed, and ready to fire as well as literally engulfed in smoke and flame as the rockets head skywards.

Israel has demonstrated great ingenuity in developing and deploying various calibres of rocket artillery. Two types are illustrated here, that at left being the LAR-160, each rocket being able to deliver a 110lb (50kg) warhead which may contain sub-munitions or high explosive over distances of up to 18 miles (30km). Now in Israeli Defence Force use, vehicle-mounted launchers can carry as many as 50 tubes but the AMX-13 chassis shown here has just 36. Greater "clout" is possessed by the 290mm MRS which has a similar range but a much heavier 705lb (320kg) HE warhead and a four-tube launcher is seen at right on a Centurion chassis.

Among the least sophisticated types of rocket artillery is South Africa's 127mm Valkiri device, shown at left at the moment of firing from a towed 12-shot launcher. Far greater degrees of both mobility and lethality are enjoyed by the 24-round launch box which can be seen at right but it does appear vulnerable to counter-attack and would probably be rendered useless by one well-aimed missile or bomb.

Shown here being fired under test conditions, the Tactical Missile System (TACMS) is now under development for service with the US Army. Designed to be launched from MLRS vehicles, one TACMS missile replaces a "six-pack" of standard MLRS rockets in the launcher unit. In service, maximum range will be of the order of 150 miles (240km) and it will initially be used to drop sub-munitions to disrupt follow-on enemy forces. Later developments are likely to result in warheads capable of destroying "hard" targets such as command bunkers as well as missile sites and air bases located far behind the forward edge of battle area.

In service with five French Army regiments, each of which has six launch vehicles, the Pluton battlefield tactical nuclear missile may carry two different types of warhead. Much less powerful than the USA's Pershing, these have a yield of either 15kT or 25kT. Range capability is dependent on which of these options is fitted, varying from 12 to 75 miles (19 to 120km). Regardless of the type of warhead, the containerised weapon is carried and fired by a vehicle which is based on an AMX-30 tank chassis.

Warhead options on the MGM-52 Lance tactical battlefield missile vary, encompassing a nuclear type with a yield of some 10kT as well as chemical and conventional devices and the contentious "neutron" or enhanced radiation bomb. With a range that varies from 45 to 75 miles (72 to 120km), Lance can be launched from the M752 amphibious tracked vehicle which is based on the M113 armoured personnel carrier. Alternatively, a lightweight towed firing platform can be used, the latter having the advantage that it is air-droppable. Launchers of both types are seen here, with the picture above showing firing crew members hurrying to set up a remote launch position.

Possessing quite exceptional accuracy, the MGM-31 Pershing II battlefield missile evolved from the earlier Pershing I/IA which was deployed in Europe with elements of both the US Army and West Germany's Luftwaffe. Offering greater range, the Mk.II version would normally carry a W-50 nuclear warhead with a yield of around 400kT. Deployment with the US Army in Europe went ahead in the mid-1980s although all 108 missiles are to be withdrawn following ratification of the Intermediate Nuclear Forces (INF) treaty which basically eliminated nuclear weapons defined as possessing medium-range. Here we see personnel of the US Army in Europe assembling a Pershing II in the field and a test shot that took place in the USA before deployment got under way.

Heavily-armoured vehicles such as main battle tanks don't have it all their own way on the modern battlefield for even the humble infantry is able to pose a serious danger to their continued well-being with weapons like the Hughes BGM-71 TOW anti-armour missile. A flexible system with land-based and airborne applications, TOW is part of the USA's Fast Attack Vehicle armament and is much feared by tank crews who could well one day become targets for this simple but extremely accurate weapon.

With the guidance wires along which steering signals are transmitted clearly visible, a Hughes BGM-71 Improved TOW missile leaves its launch tube and accelerates towards a distant target. Easy to aim and fire, graphic proof of the devastating power of this weapon is provided by the view of a tank engulfed in smoke and flame after taking a direct hit.

08FF07

One of several light tracked reconnaissance vehicles that comprise the Scorpion family, Striker is a dedicated tank-buster which carries a five-round launcher for Swingfire anti-tank missiles. Examples of this weapon are seen being fired in the two accompanying pictures which show Striker in readiness, with the launch bin in the elevated position. Wire-guided, Swingfire has a maximum range of 4,375 yards (4,000m) and may be fired by means of remote control from a position up to 110 yards (100m) away from the vehicle.

mée de TERRE
ATC

Tank crews might be excused for thinking that the odds are likely to be very heavily weighed against them in any future conflict. As far as missile threats are concerned there is certainly an awesome array of weapons on offer, including the Euromissile HOT which is seen being fired from a Gazelle of the French Army and a German Army Bolkow Bo.105. Vehicles like the eight-wheeled MOWAG Piranha may also carry HOT.

Braced to absorb the impetus of launch, a US Army soldier keeps his eye firmly on the sighting device as a Dragon anti-tank missile emerges at the start of its flight to a target (left), while other Dragon-armed troops (above and right) run through the launch procedure. Introduced into operational service almost 20 years ago, Dragon is now the subject of an improvement effort aimed at enhancing its armour-penetration potential and accuracy.

248 W 93

Versatility is also a keyword of the Euromissile Milan which is in service with a long list of customers around the world. Man-portable and vehicle-mounted options may be employed but no air-launched version has been developed and none now seems likely to be. Initially evolved as a day weapon, Milan may be fired at night through the addition of a thermal imaging sighting device. Like many similar weapons, guidance is by means of fine wires which automatically relay steering commands to the weapon's control surfaces. All the operator has to do is ensure that the chosen target remains centred in the cross-hairs of the sight and Milan will home unerringly.

Among the most potent in the man-portable anti-tank weapon category is the Swedish RBS56 Bill which can also be easily fitted to a wide variety of vehicles. Like TOW, guidance signals are transmitted by wire, the operator simply having to keep the crosshairs on the target to ensure that a hit ensues. Unlike TOW, it is a top-attack device, which flies a few feet above the line-of-sight and has a canted-down warhead triggered by a proximity fuse. In this way, explosive energy is directed into the top of a tank where the armour is thinner and angled to defeat a direct attack.

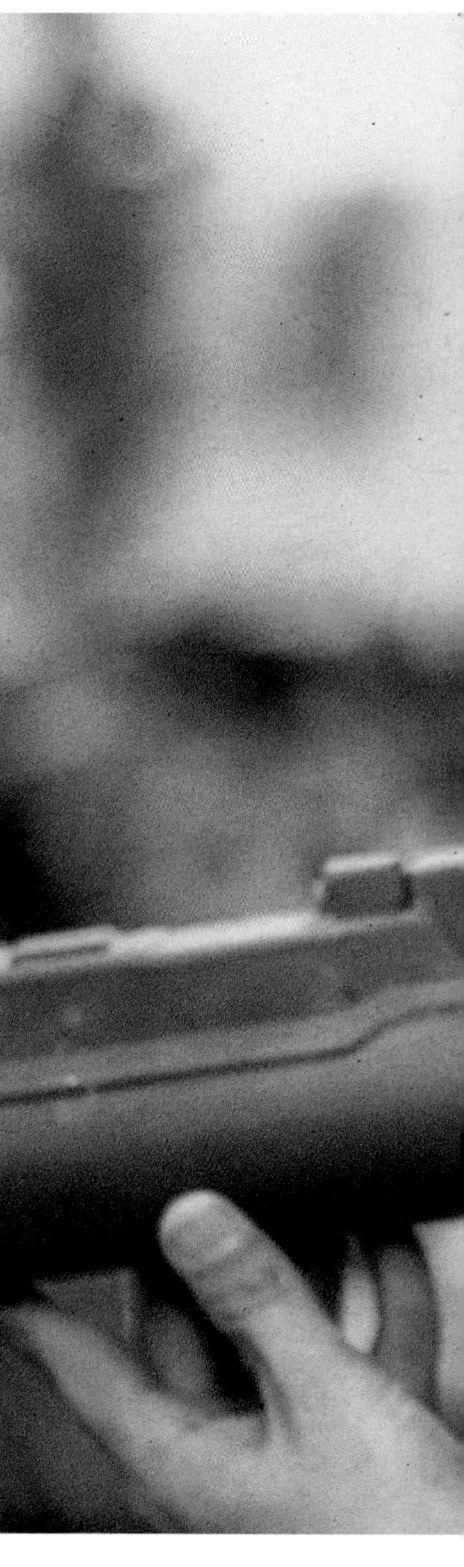

Of all the many man-portable general purpose devices, the LAW (Light Assault Weapon) may be the most simple of all and could be described as being a "fire and forget" system in that, once used, it is simply thrown away. Here, camouflage-daubed soldiers of the US Army move into action with LAW.

HORTON

The SMAW (Shoulder-launched Multi-purpose Assault Weapon) is another device that is now entering service with the US armed forces and one that possesses a reasonable punch. Comparison with LAW soon reveals that it is more sophisticated and one doubts if troops would be encouraged to dispose of it after use as it is reloadable. As well as in the anti-armour role, SMAW is used to attack bunkers and defensive positions and can be thought of as "man-portable artillery".

When it comes to liaison and reconnaissance duties, these can be fulfilled by a variety of vehicles in a variety of configurations. Most are only modestly armed and armoured, speed and mobility being key design factors and they are portrayed here by the French VBL (far right) and American HMMWV (right) vehicles. Inevitably, some of these support vehicle classes do possess greater firepower, the "Hummer" depicted below being typical in that it has a ground-launched variant of the Hellfire missile on a rail launcher.

Multi-purpose equipment looks like being the way ahead in a time of defence cuts and the Swiss/American Air Defence/Anti-Tank System looks as if it will fit the bill nicely, in that it seems to offer an effective way to counter the threat posed by air and armour in a single package. Missiles are the key item of armament, with homing being accomplished with the aid of a laser guidance beam emitted from the launcher itself. In the pictures above and at far left, test missiles are fired while its "go anywhere" value is shown left as an American version on a Bradley chassis splashes its way across a river bed. The electro-optical search and tracking system is based on the same system used by the Apache attack helicopter.

Efforts to counter the threat posed by tactical air power have seen the deployment of a number of air defence weapons systems, with both guns and missiles being used. Roland is an example of the latter category, this Franco-German project having achieved great success on the export market as well as at home. In French service, Roland is mounted on a modified AMX-30 MBT chassis (far left) while Germany has chosen the Marder as a basis for its system (above and left). A pair of missiles are usually carried in the launch position with a further eight missiles in four-round drum magazines housed in the hull. Two radars are fitted, the upper dish-type antenna being for general surveillance and the other for precise target tracking.

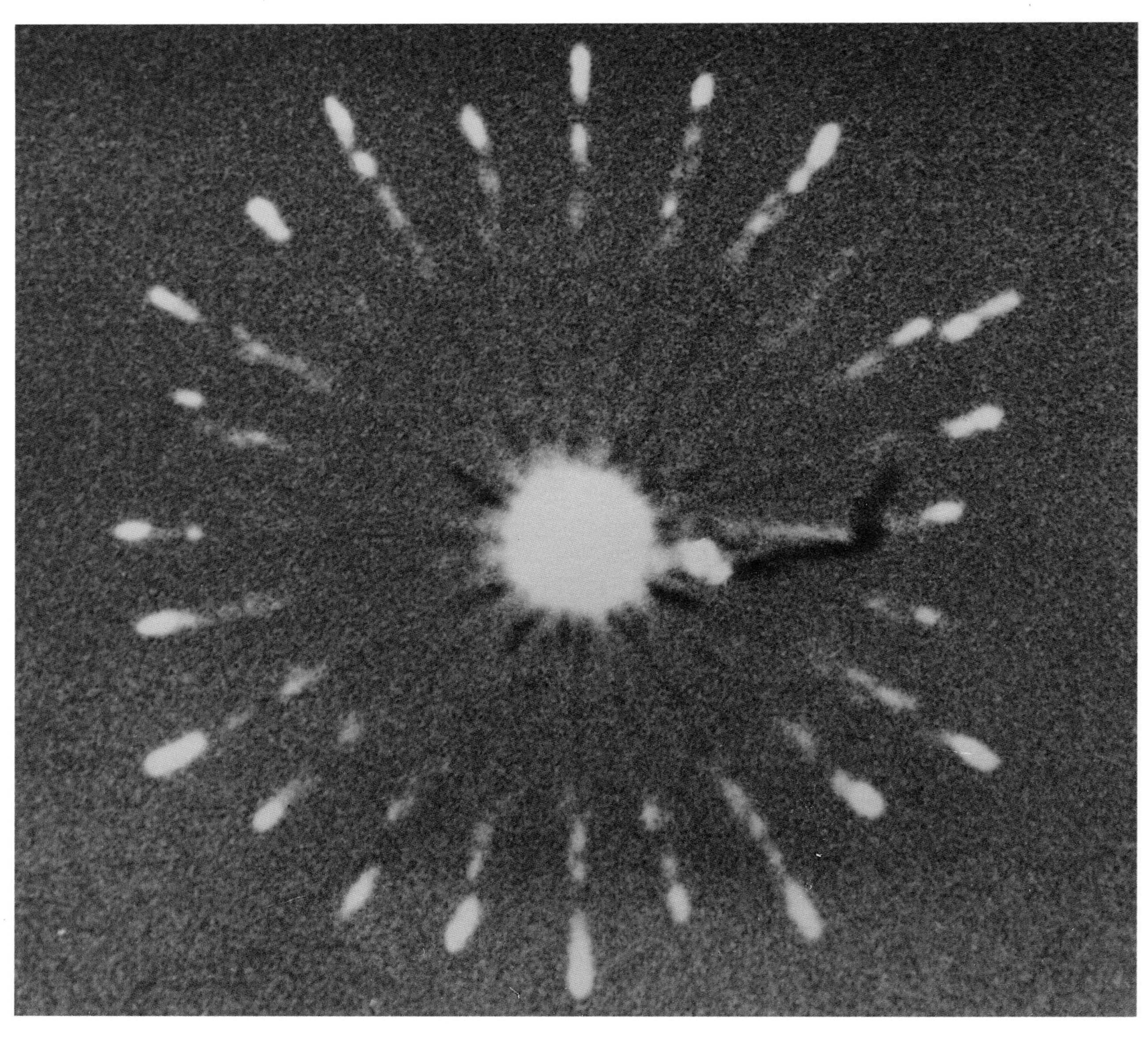

One important customer for the Franco/German Roland air defence missile is the United States which conducted firing trials using an XM985 tracked vehicle (below and right). An experimental concept based on the M109 self-propelled 155mm howitzer chassis, it was not adopted for operational use but test firings confirmed Roland's worth and resulted in several unmanned drone targets being destroyed at the White Sands missile range (left).

Originally evolved for South Africa as the Cactus, France has since adopted this air defence missile system itself as the Crotale. In service, a typical battery consists of a pair of P4R firing vehicles, each with four containerised missiles (left and below left), and a P4R vehicle with acquisition radar. Other armoured vehicles such as the MOWAG Shark (right) can also be used to carry Crotale. Continuous improvement has enabled the system to remain effective and new variants include the Shahine (below right), a six-missile version developed for Saudi Arabia.

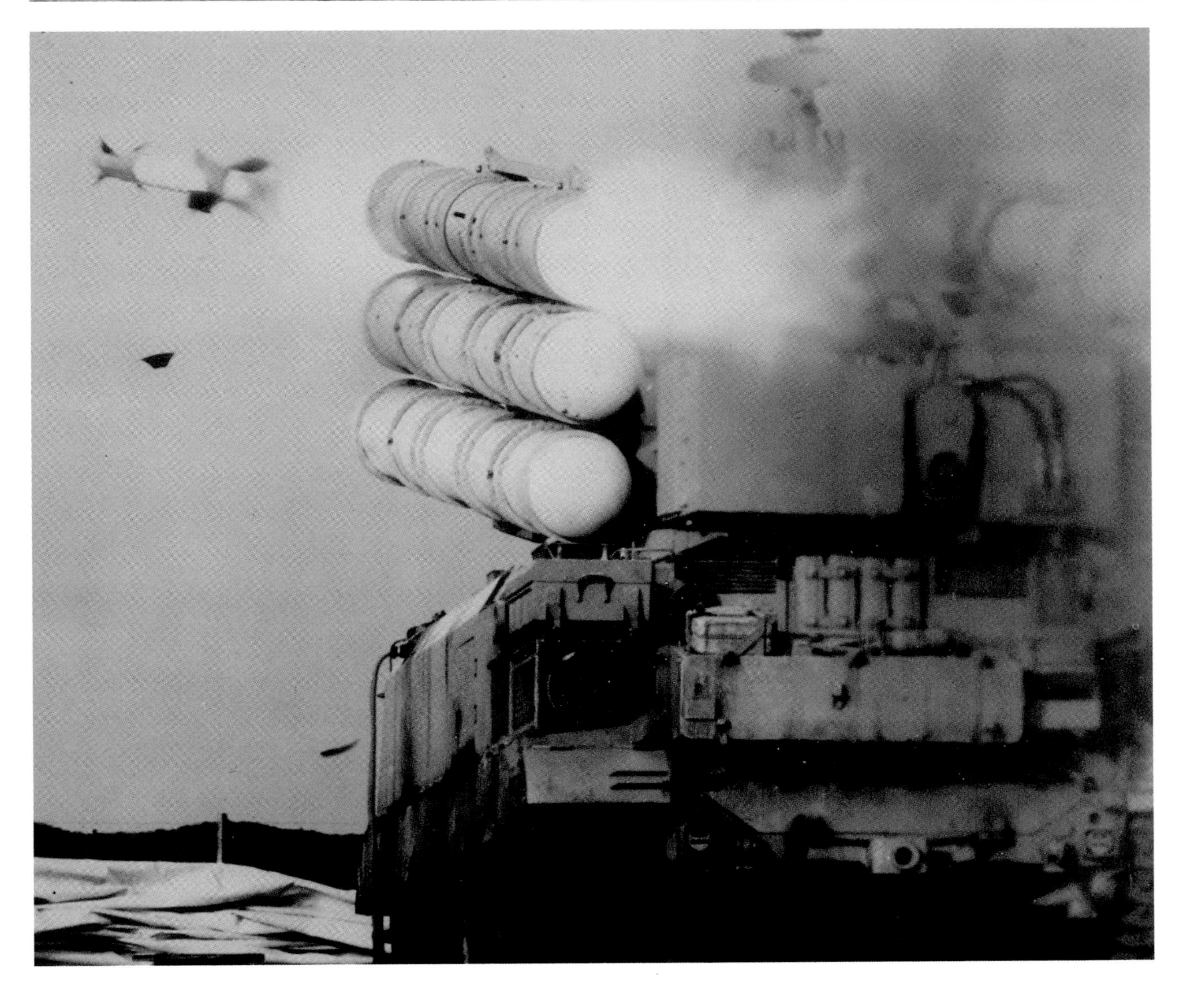

The simple but effective Chapparal air defence system has been in US Army service for many years. Four Sidewinder heat-seeking missiles (originally developed for air-to-air use) are mounted on a tracked chassis derived from the M-113 personnel carrier. Upgraded with night-vision equipment and new missile seeker heads, Chapparal is still a potent threat to the strike pilot.

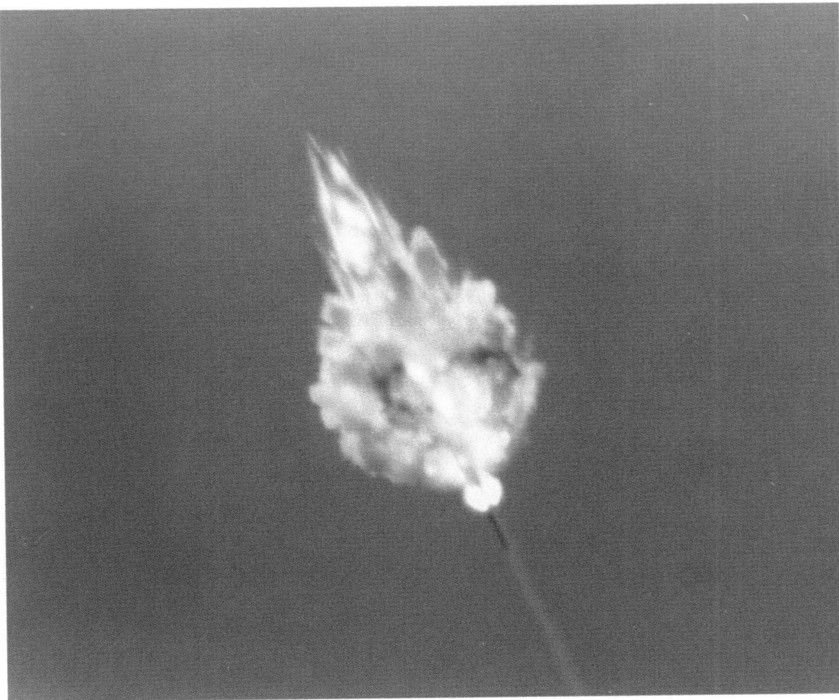

For use against aircraft and tactical missiles, Patriot is now in service with elements of the US Army and has shown a high kill probability in live firing tests conducted at White Sands missile range in New Mexico. Radar-guided, it has greater mobility than the Nike Hercules which it replaces. Shown here seconds after launch, its potential effectiveness was revealed in striking fashion in 1986 when it successfully intercepted a Lance tactical ballistic missile at White Sands, the sequence of pictures on this page showing the moment of impact (top), warhead detonation (centre) and the disabled Lance plunging back to earth (bottom).

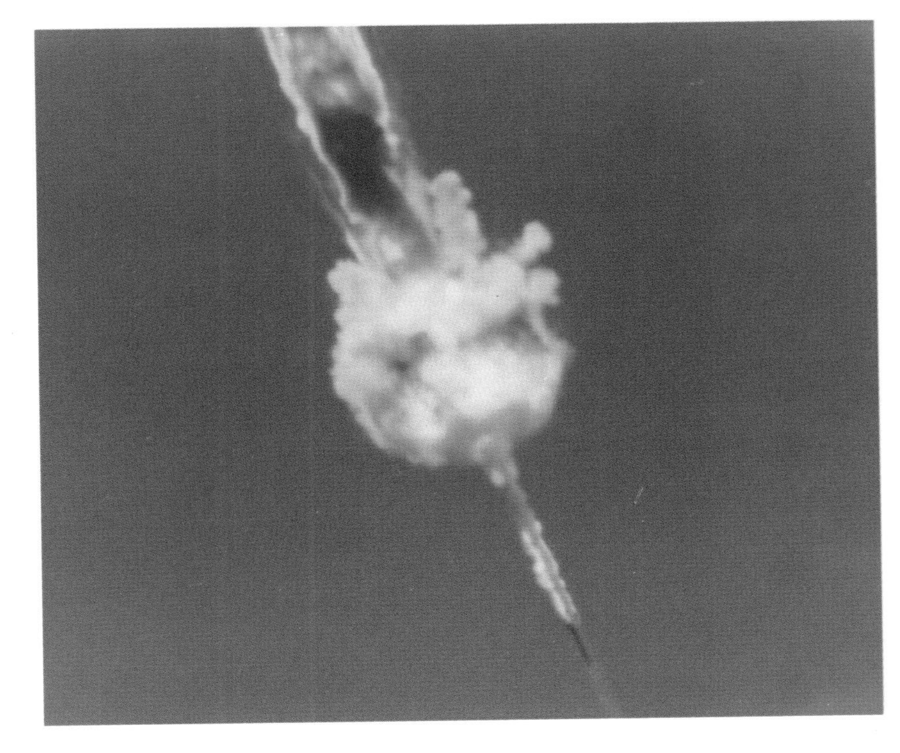

Proving its value in combat in the 1982 battles for the Falkland Islands, Rapier may be fired from fixed launchers (left and far left), target tracking and missile control being accomplished remotely from a well-camouflaged site (above). Responsible for the destruction of several enemy aircraft in 1982, Rapier is in service with several countries around the world.

DANTE

OPEN
CLOSED

A logical development of the towed Rapier, the tracked version can be ready to fire within 30 seconds of coming to a stop and is operated by a crew of three, one of whom is seen in the fairly cramped confines of the armoured cab. Eight missiles is the full load and all command and control functions are fully integrated in what is clearly a highly mobile piece of kit.

The American M113 armoured personnel carrier has been extensively modified since it entered service in 1960, one variation on the theme being illustrated here. Intended to fulfil the forward- area air defence task, the M163 has a 20mm Vulcan cannon and undoubtedly poses a threat to any flying machine unfortunate or unwise enough to come within range.

BSI

As well as the more complex and sophisticated air defence weapons such as Patriot, Hawk and Roland, a number of simple to operate man-portable types are now in widespread service with armies around the globe. Matra's Mistral is typical of this category of weapon and, like most of them, is a "heat seeker", designed to home on infra-red energy such as that emanating from jet engines. Applications also embrace an air-launched model suitable for helicopter self-defence in and around a battlefield.

Used in combat by Mujahideen rebel forces in Afghanistan, Stinger is known to have been responsible for destroying numerous fixed and rotary-wing craft. Production has mainly been of the portable shoulder-fired versions (far left and above) but it is also used on the Avenger air defence system (centre).

One of the most lethal types of man-portable anti-aircraft missile is Stinger, shown at the instant of launch in the picture above. Homing on infra-red heat emitted by a target, Stinger quickly accelerates to about Mach 2 and some idea of this weapon's destructive ability may be gleaned from the views on the right which illustrate the fiery end of an obsolete UH-1 Iroquois helicopter during a live-firing test.

The Canadian LAV25 chassis has also provided a starting point for a class of vehicles engaged in forward area air defence duties with elements of the United States Marines. The Stinger infra-red homing surface-to-air missile forms part of the Blazer turret package which is depicted at right and below right. Backed up by a rapid-firing General Electric 25mm rotary cannon, it could easily spoil the day of any enemy pilot foolhardy enough to come within range while the competing system shown below is also clearly capable of inflicting serious damage.

3-B-36

(Overleaf) The US Marine Corps is unique in that land, sea and air warfare are all incorporated in the one service. All elements are evident in this study of a beach assault exercise, the AH-1T SeaCobra gunships providing a measure of aerial cover as troops fan out after leaving the LVTP7 vehicles which ferried them from ship to shore. Out of sight, Marine jet attack aircraft like the Harrier II and Hornet will also be busy, attacking enemy installations and undertaking close air support in the first critical minutes of the landing.

US Marine Corps doctrine lays heavy emphasis on this force being the first to fight and they are widely recognised as amphibious warfare experts. Among vehicles now in use by the Marine Corps is the amphibious LVTP7 shown above in sea-borne 'swimming' mode. This troop carrier will spearhead any invasion and gun-toting soldiers are seen leaving one at left, as they rush to establish a defensive perimeter at the start of a beach assault while another example kicks up the sand as it ploughs its way out of the sea.

L 15

A huge sheet of spray erupts as an LVTP7 leaves the ramp of an amphibious assault ship and heads towards the shore (left), where a machine gun nest manned by two Marines maintains a perimeter guard as the beach-head is secured (below). In the background, an LVTP7 stands waiting, its job temporarily done.

Although tanks are invariably associated with scenes like that depicting a Challenger in mock battle (upper left), the reality is very different and much of the time is spent waiting around for the call to arms. The other two views are typical of the inactivity and are of the earlier Chieftain.

06FA72

Some may think that tank crews have an easy time of it but that is far from true. Each shell visible in this picture will have to be loaded into these tanks by hand, manoeuvring the heavy, cumbersome rounds through a small hatch.

Dominated by the business end of a 105mm M68 gun, the study (left) of the turret of an M1 Abrams MBT reveals the slab-sided contours to advantage, smoke generators also being visible at the extreme right. Well protected it may be but it is far from comfortable as the other two pictures show only too well. The view at right shows an M1 driver with protective kit which is most certainly needed since he has to manoeuvre this cumbersome vehicle from a position right below the gun (see below). On metalled roads, operation is probably not too unpleasant but in the desert, where dust is an ever-present source of irritation, inadequate dress would soon ruin his day.

002

425

One of the most unusual US Army outfits is "OpFor" which is equipped with a number of redundant M551 Sheridan light tanks that have been modified to replicate Soviet types of armoured fighting vehicle. In altered form, they are used to train Army combat echelons in Warsaw Pact battle tactics and three of these look-alike vehicles are portrayed here. Reading clockwise from the top left, they are intended to portray the T-72 MBT, the ZSU-23-4 Shilka anti-aircraft mobile gun system and the BMP infantry combat vehicle.

Bathed in the eerie red light produced by flares, the snow-covered terrain visible in this night picture of a small village shows little evidence of military might but forces are most certainly out there somewhere.

(Overleaf) Combat by night is always a spectacular sight as this somewhat bizarre picture shows. Illuminated with the aid of slow-burning parachute flares, a distant target is a focal point for concentrated fire.

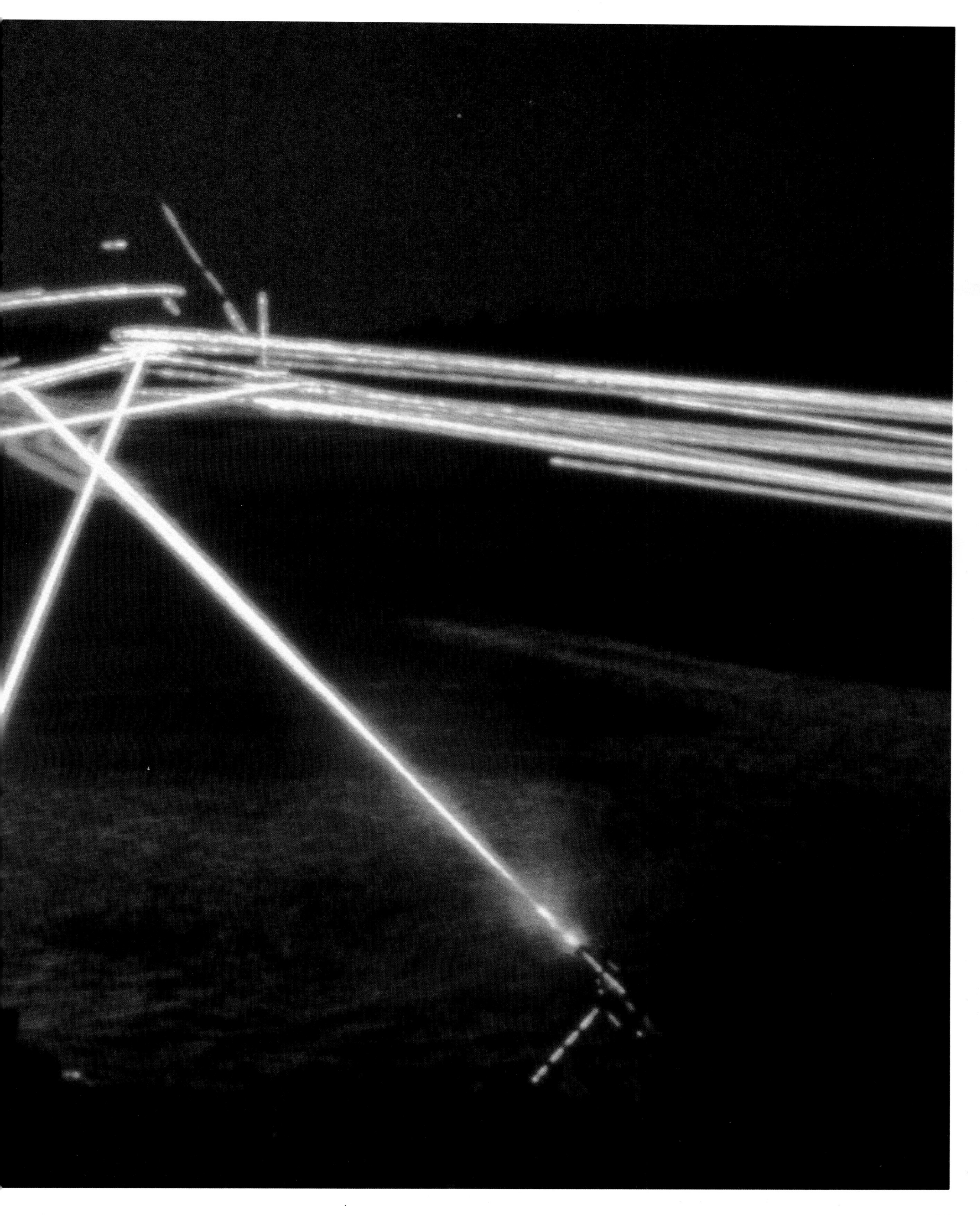

(Previous page) Evidence of spin-stabilisation of a shell by a rifled-barrel can be easily seen in this dramatic study of a British Army Chieftain firing its big 120mm cannon during a night exercise.

Desert terrain is in many ways still perceived as being an ideal habitat for the main battle tank, allowing it to take advantage of speed and mobility although it does not necessarily offer much in the way of good cover. In these views, which depict variants of the American M60, US Army examples are shown on desert training (left and below) while the remaining picture is of Israeli machines which are fitted with Blazer "add-on" reactive armour boxes.

Seen against a backdrop of snow-covered countryside, a gaggle of US Army M60 main battle tanks pause to await fresh instructions, their road lights glowing brightly in the otherwise gloomy conditions of a typical European winter's day while another M60 spews out a thick cloud of black exhaust smoke as it hurries down a south German highway.

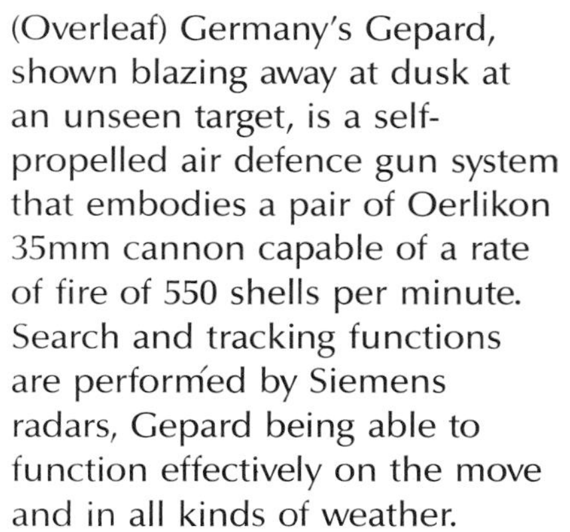

(Overleaf) Germany's Gepard, shown blazing away at dusk at an unseen target, is a self-propelled air defence gun system that embodies a pair of Oerlikon 35mm cannon capable of a rate of fire of 550 shells per minute. Search and tracking functions are performed by Siemens radars, Gepard being able to function effectively on the move and in all kinds of weather.